FORBIDDEN THOUGHTS

MyStique

FORBIDDEN THOUGHTS

©2016 MyStique

Forbidden Thoughts

In Shock

Gone

I Love

Fantasy

Borrowed Time

Nostalgia

Sleepless Nights

Soul Cry

Captured

If Things Were Different

Paint My Pussy

With You

I Need You

Fienden'

Fill Me Up

My Fix

My Pussy Is Calling

Won't Waste a Drop

Splash

Nothing Better

Day Dreaming

Jealous

Belong

Our Love

Forbidden Thoughts..

Flood my mind

Every encounter plays back like a porno

Making my muscles start to twitch

Got me crossing and re-crossing my legs

Like that will stop my juices from flowing

Amazed that just a thought

Can bring back the sensation

I can feel your hands cupping my breasts

The hairs on your chest

Your manhood deep inside

Stroking brings tears to my eyes

Your lips closed around my nipples

Your tongue sucking and licking from left to right

Giving the girls the attention that they love

That Rock Hard Dick invades my tunnel

Making me scream

Grabbing on your arms

Running my hands over your muscles

Grind Deeper, Harder

Stroke Faster, Stronger

I Want all of Him

I Need all of You

Forbidden Thoughts of My Muse

Can you feel me sucking on that dick

Til he Rock Hard

Sitting on him slowly

My back to you as I glide down

Pussy muscles squeezing .. choking

Pulling you deeper as I dip it low

Your hands grabbing my cheeks

Bouncing me on that dick

Two fingers take over my clit

Driving my senses to the verge of explosion

You pull me back to you holding me against your chest

Cupping my breasts as we Grind together

I turn around as you put my legs on your shoulders

That dick so deep inside

Could we get any closer

You standing up in this pussy

Banging that dick in my box

My heart racing

Juices flowing

I think I'm in shock

My mind takes me back to a place

My own piece of heaven

A week long rendezvous

I had you all to my self

Early Morning Love

Just Because Quick Fucks

Late Night Love Sessions

Wild and Loud

From the bedroom to the bathroom sink

Showering to do it all again

Makes me think back to our first weekend road trip

Too excited to be disappearing with you

No one knowing where we're going

Or what we getting in to

You got all inside me...entered my domain

Took over my vitals .. my being

Made love to me for the first time

And had me Gone

I LOVE.... That pick me up and PUT IT DOWN phy-
sique

That make me weak in the knees

Mind Blowing

Body Controlling Top of the lungs

Noise Making

Neighbors Damn Sure Know Ya Name

SEX GAME

That can't get enough

Fiendin' for your touch

Half Crazy cuz I don't want to share LOVE

That feel Soooooo Good stroking

That make you tear up

Driving soooooo deep

I can feel you in my lungs

Pumping oxygen straight to my heart

Making sure that I breath

SEX GAME OFF THE CHARTS

Make you not want to leave LOVE

That walk around the room flipping

Slip and sliding

Grab my hair and smack my ass

Make me scream

Make me cream LOVE

I love how you LOVE

Fantasy

Flashbacks of previous encounters clutter my mind

Wishing I could rewind time

Back to when we were

Somewhat carefree

Enjoying each other's company

Our first time

Is etched in my memory

As if you were the only one

Taking control of my body and my heart follows

I want to be where you are

Fantasies of my Love

BORROWED TIME

You were mine

If only for a moment

Our time was magical

Had me in my feelings

Thinking about what ifs...

Trying to determine if it's real

Or just a game

I can't complain though

For my heart wants who it wants

And my passion is awakened in a simple touch

You make my love come down in immeasurable pleasures

Satisfying every part of me

You are my sorcerer

And I am your genie

Make your wishes be known

All is not lost

When I have the memory of you

Etched in to my soul

I go back to those memories and think....

Sexing you for the first time
Was all that I imagined
Feeling you stroking me
Holding me
Your lips on my skin
Tantalizing tongue games
My pussy gets wet at the thought

Wanting to feel your hardness
My juices start to flow
Fingers explore my honey

My legs wrapped around your waist
Anticipating your entry
Fireworks in my mind
All night love session
With an intermittent break

Dick Game on a thousand
Muscles sore from pure pleasure
GOOD MORNING LOVE
Letting me know it wasn't a dream

Just memories...played back

Nostalgia

Sleepless nights...

Tossing and turning...

Visions of you in my head

In my bed

Wrapped in my embrace

Intertwined....

Thighs hugging your sides

As you cradle my legs in the bend of your arms

Driving deep within

Slowly.. Stroking

In and out

I feel every part of you

Moans escape my lips

I can't help but make love sounds and love faces

The pleasure is Real

THE PASSION EXPLOSIVE

Legs trembling as you speed up

and Grind harder

Ready to release your sons and daughters

Make my dreams come true

When you give me

a Little You

Soul Cry

I can't shed tears for what could have been
I smile at the thought of what could become
A love unmatched by any
A bond intertwined in more than just lust
Truth.... for our hearts speak to each other
Reminding us to never let go

For how can my soul be attracted to yours so strongly
Drawing us to one another
Subconsciously
Only something so Real
Can feel so Right

Yet at the end of the night
I have to hold in my tears
And fight
For my love cannot be fulfilled...

First he stole my heart

Took my mind by the hand and molded me

Feelings don't change

Just circumstances

What is to become of us

FRIENDS

LOVERS

Why not both

Maybe one day

An Acquaintance

Chance encounter

Bought us back into each other's realms

I can't let it go this time

We need to explore these feelings

These slight but temporary dealings have me open

Heart stole

Mind gone

Lost control

His goal...

CAPTURED

If things were different would they still be the same let
me explain...
I mean, could I believe that if it was you and me
I wouldn't be deceived

In times past we've both done things
But time's changed me and I want more than what we
were...
Not to go to the extreme cuz I realize now
I'm content just with me

But would love having you beside me...
You being you
Enjoying each other
My Friend and My Lover
The best combination of pleasure
Submission of will as we explore together
Senses aroused in a caress or a kiss
Long lasting Love making
Moans from my lips to your ears...yet everyone can hear
You turn me into a lioness
Purring for My Lion

My pussy throbs at the thought of him
Running thru my mind
All Day and All Night

My thoughts bring back memories
Of you filling me up
Muscles contracting

The throbbing gets stronger
At the sight of him
I smile

Wanting to hold him
Feel the hardness of him
Ready to invade my pussy

I lick my lips wanting to give him a kiss
Lick him up and down
Tongue twirl on the tip

Lips wrapped around
Feed him to me
Cum inside...
Paint My Pussy

I look at that dick and play with my pussy....
You make me cum soooo hard
I need to feel the curve of him

The length
The width
The stroke
Of him

I need to feel each stroke
As you enter and drive deeper into my depths
Making my love come down in waves
Take me to a higher plateau
In the bliss of our love making
You are the memory that I can't seem to forget
Nor do I want to

For all of my thoughts are filled with you

Being with you

Laying with you

Staying with you

I NEED YOU

deep inside me

stroking my walls into submission

Legs trembling

my juices flowing

slurping on ya dick as you go in and out

muscles contracting pulling you deeper

I NEED YOU

paint my walls with your ecstasy

driving my passion beyond depths ever reached

I NEED YOU

My pussy calling you boo I need to feel you
I want to feel your lips leaving trails of kisses
from my neck to my nipples

I love when you close your lips around them
and suck on them
Feel your tongue doing circles
While your dick circles my opening

We both creaming from anticipation
Wrapping my legs around your waist

Pulling you close
You digging deeper

Fill me up baby
Give me those babies

I need all of you to give my all to you
That is my craving

My Appetite can't be satisfied

Until you fill me up

Anticipation got me anxious I can't sleep thru the night

My mind racing trying to imagine

Our love making

My body craves your touch

My soul craves your presence

I need that Act Right

That put me to sleep

Sweet Dreaming of the morning after love

I can't get enuff

I love them chocolate covered nuts

You are my Addiction

Fiending for that Dick

Needing you next to me
Feeling you sexing me
Is all I think about

Needing that ecstasy
You exploring my body
Is all that I dream about

Your touch is magnetic
Drawing me to you
The attraction has me transfixed

I feel your life force
With every thought
Is a memory of what once was

I Need that feeling back
Going thru withdrawal
Trying to refrain

You are my drug of choice
My Addiction
MY FIX

My pussy is calling you
Can you hear her whispers
Inviting you to Cum inside

Telling you that it's okay
To get comfortable
and make yourself at home

She can serve you up

Breakfast..
Lunch..
Dinner..
Desert..

And that late night treat
Satisfying that sweet tooth
Butter Cream filled Chocolate Kiss

Waiting for your Almond Joy
To part her creamy lips
Slide that Snickers Bar to me

So that I can satisfy my hunger...

You don't even understand how bad I want to feel him

deep inside me filling me up.

I want to put my lips all around him and feel him sliding
down my throat.

Make my legs shake as you drive deeper into my treasure
box.

Your legs tremble at the flick of my tongue teasing the
tip.

My lips...both sets hold on to what they want

The grip...unshakeable

Satisfying Sensations

Unmistakable

Give me all of you

I Won't Waste A Drop

SPLASH

Beware of the waterfall

Totally overtaking you as you glide inside its folds

Monsoon drenched
Hurricane Katrina wrapped around you
Consuming all of your energy
As you try to ride the tides

Left stroke
Right stroke
Back stroke

There's no escaping

Sugar walls got you drowning

Splashing down on you

SPLASH

As the lights dim and I light some candles
The music starts to play
I straddle you
Undressing you
Your shirt hits the floor and
Your pants follow suit
Sliding boxer briefs over your manhood
Admiring my view
Taking him into my mouth
Tasting your sweetness
The aroma of your maleness
Intoxicating…my senses in over drive
Your touch makes me weak
As you guide me to ride him
Bounce my hips on that dick
Slow Grind Whind
Your tongue teasing my nipples
Damn you feel so good
Feeling your depth all in my guts
Hitting all G spots
Got us both bustin' Nuts

Ain't Nothing Better
Than when we cumin together
Passion Unbridled
Shared between lovers

Can you feel her squeezing you

Trying to drain you of all your life form

Wanting all of your maleness to fill my
womb

Allow me to take over creation of an
other life

Our DNA intermingle

Creating a little you inside me

The miracle that love can make

That is my dream

DAYDREAMING

Jealous

I want what I want But can't have you
For, we both are forbidden fruit
Not wanting to hurt feelings But my heart is missing you
I feel trapped and just want to escape
If only for one night
Take you away from everything and everyone
Take another flight To that forbidden city
Where we can escape to pleasure each other
My memories are filled with us
Being more than friends but lovers
Jealous cuz I know what I'm missing
She's getting what's meant for me
Wishing we were together So I could feel that ecstasy
That oh so good love making
That has me all up in a daze
That Act Right got my mind Running thru a maze
Trying to figure out a way To get where I belong
Jealous cuz I want what I want
And the feeling is so strong
Jealous cuz I want to trade places
Knowing that I should be
Where she is... pleasing you
And giving you all of me
But I can't...SO I'm Jealous

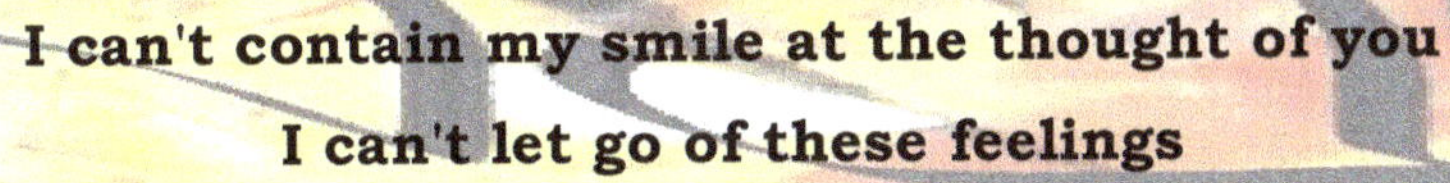

I can't contain my smile at the thought of you
I can't let go of these feelings

They're too deep rooted
No one will understand but me and you
That what we share is true

True friendship
True Love
And Lovemaking

True Bond
Something that can't be broken

With all these truths

How can we go wrong

WE too strong

And with you

My heart
My body
My Soul
Belong

The love we share has a chance to blossom
I can be free again

To express and receive
All that I have stored up

Overflowing and ready to flood your existence
My heart has been released from the chains

Binding and holding me in place
Ready to explore what our relationship really means

Our bond being what it is
It can only be something Sweet

Spoil me with your candy
Fill my cavity

Waiting patiently to be...

Fixed

ACKNOWLEDGEMENTS

Ah, Where to Start, I have been working on this collection of poetry for 8 months now and I am so excited to say that I am finished and ready to share my gift with the world. This is my baby, my first attempt at sharing with the masses my love for writing. I have a select few of people who have been in my corner from start to finish of this project, and I could not go without giving them their props.

FIRST ALL PRAISE IS DUE TO GOD

FOR GIVING ME THE GIFT

Secondly, My Mother for believing in my gift

And always encouraging me to KEEP WRITING

Thirdly, My Sounding Board, My Loves

My MUSE-J(S)B

Nikki Cowell

Mrs. Shanette Jesse

Jaymee Williams

From reading every poem to rereading to make sure that everything was flowing, my squad has been my peace of mind and motivation. The finished product definitely has their finishing touches and I am proud to present My First Collection.

Special Thanks for the Artwork throughout the book goes to Shiree Bass-Henry.

I hope you all enjoyed the Forbidden!! Look out for Forbidden Thoughts II and other collections to follow. I am SO INSPIRED.

MyStique

A Mystery Wrapped in Brown Skin

Whose love for writing

started at an early age.

Spotlight is not my Claim

Sharing my Passion is my Aim

Evidenced by the mystery of my name.